The cover shows Edward Furlong age 17
with one of his larger bee colonies.

This is a second edition as a few
additional thoughts need to be added
since I'm now 93.5 years old.

TABLE OF CONTENTS

Preface   And a warning..................3

Chapter 1   Youth, bees, and health.....10

Chapter 2   Becoming an auditor.........21

Chapter 3   Potable water................29

Chapter 4   Bread to eat...................35

Chapter 5   Finding high protein..........42

Chapter 6   Careful measuring...........48

Chapter 7   Fruits and vegetables......56

Chapter 8   Supplements.................64

Chapter 9   Nuts, bees and drugs........71

Chapter 10   The end of bees.............77

PREÇACE
And a Warning

Who am I to write this advisory for others? Well, I'm 91¾ as I begin to write this short book. In the latest Annual Record (125 pages) of my college at university there were 58 obituaries. 57 died younger than my age, only one was older. He died at age 96. So I must be doing something right, and if diet has anything to do with old age, at least as I'm still surviving I thought you might like to know how I keep my body and brain going.

I believe it is important for you not to skip what I have to say next.

In 2005 (when I was 85) I decided that if I followed the usual procedure and left everything to my wife (that we did not already share), then on her death it would go to our son and on his death to his wife and on her death to their three children. By then there would be next to nothing left. Here's why. A will has to be probated by the courts or banks will not release funds.

For a will to be probated a lawyer takes over administration of the 'estate' and prepares it for probate. By law a lawyer has 1 year to complete this before submitting it to the probate court. So lawyers customarily take a year to do this. The lawyer charges a fee for every disbursement made, a fee for every receipt taken, and annually a percentage fee for all the assets, and all the liabilities. Added to this are probate court costs and legal costs for court appearances. All these charges would be repeated four times before the remainder reached the grandchildren. You can see there would be little left for them. Although our assets were not huge they represented our lifetimes' work. So I decided to set up an Intervivos (Latin for living) Joint Spousal Trust.

I drafted and wrote the 26 pages of the trust myself and persuaded the government to permit me to buy and use the software program lawyers use. The intent was to transfer our family assets into the trust, so I could set it up exactly as I wanted without high fees, and complete it promptly. But I had only worked with the program about a week mostly spent learning to use it, when the government suddenly decreed that only lawyers would be allowed to own and operate the system starting two days from then. This put extreme pressure on me, although fortunately Sean, our eldest grandson, came to help me. Between us we mastered the system and transferred the assets into the Trust with about two hours to spare. Now, neither my wife nor I have assets, so there is no need for wills. When we die the Trust will just carry on as if nothing had happened. Of course we still have income, but it comes from the Trust.

Why tell you all this? Because about ten days later as I was talking on the phone suddenly my speech was slurred, I could no longer control my tongue properly to pronounce words. After an hour or so I partially recovered, but there were brief relapses in the next few days. So I visited my doctor. I had listed dates and times of these occurrences, which I read to him. He quickly picked up his phone and spoke a few words, then told me to have myself taken to the nearby hospital at once. A nurse was waiting with a wheelchair and took me to the ultrasound department where I was immediately body scanned ahead of all the waiting people. The result was (because I was a complete vegetarian) all my arteries and organs were completely clear of any clots so it wasn't a heart attack I had suffered. Next I had a CAT (computed axial tomography) scan of my brain. I was not told the results but a hospital doctor said he would prescribe a drug. I said 'no thanks, I don't take drugs' so he said 'aspirin?' I said 'ok' 'what strength?' '325' 'take one a day.' 2 days later I was taken to my doctor again. He told me it was a minor stroke. At once I stopped taking aspirin. It's a blood thinner. I did not want more leaking blood around my brain.

I was then sent to a neurologist, taking my DVD brain scan (unseen by me) with me. He kindly showed me the scan on his computer and said my stopping the aspirin was a smart thing to do. There were two small white dots, one on each side of my brain. He said 'that's new blood. When you age your brain shrinks inside your scalp. 2 small blood vessels have ruptured.' He wanted to have 2 more scans, one in 2 weeks, another a month later. I said no. He said 'I agree it will give you cancer down the road, but you're nearly 90 so how long have you got anyway.' I have never had the extra scans. Now that I knew what the problem was, - extreme mental stress - I made every effort to relax the tension that I felt, and 7 years later fortunately no further attacks have occurred. What I had suffered was apparently called a T I A (transient ischemic attack). From the Internet I learned that a minor one such as I had is usually followed a little later by a massive one, generally fatal.

What you'll see on the next page is the most frightening picture I have ever seen. Here's what Science says about it:

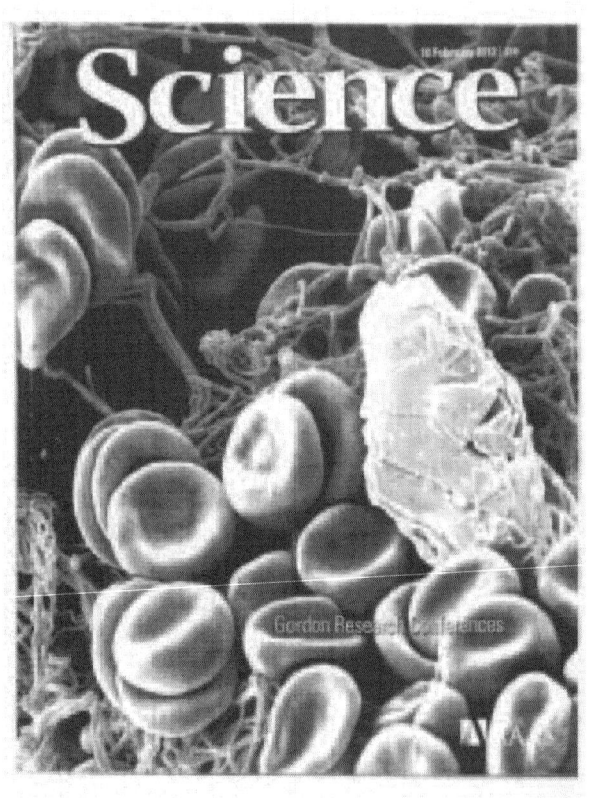

Colourized scanning electron micrograph of a blood clot removed from a patient with acute myocardial infarction, showing the fibrin meshwork (brown) with trapped red blood cells (average ~7 micrometers across) and a cholesterol crystal (yellow).

Remember that because of my vegetarian diet which I am detailing for you in this little book I had completely clear arteries and organs at age 85.

CHAPTER K

Youth, bees, and health

As a youth I was a country boy. The house had a couple of acres, a little greenhouse about the size of a small bedroom, 3 feet below ground and about 4 feet of glass above it. That was useful to give plants an early start. We grew all our own vegetables, as the subsoil was clay with good black topsoil. We had a cold room with many shelves where we put fruit and vegetables to use during winter. I always ate brown bread and carefully cut off all the fat from bacon or any other meat.

I kept bees in the orchard and sat in the trees eating the various apples, pears, greengages, plums, and watched the bees in my various hives working. If you tipped them gently from the back you could judge how much nectar/honey there was until they became too heavy to lift. I also kept goats, geese, chickens, and we had lots of dogs and cats. As my goats multiplied from 3 to 5, my father grew fed up with them and sold the lot at the local market. I was not too pleased as he got no more for 5 than I had paid for 3.

I used to cycle 8 miles to high school every day, weather permitting, and was driven there by car when it didn't. The cycling must have given me strong legs, as I became a good distance runner but not good at other track and field or sports. When I got to university I became a rower and rowed in an 8 for my college - legs again using a sliding seat. Because the river was narrow for all the 8s, we tried to physically bump the boat ahead of us. In 4 days of races our crew bumped the one ahead each day. So I must have done my bit.

I brought a hive of bees to university with me as I thought they would do well in suburban gardens. I doubt many kept bees in their rooms in the 800-year history of the university. The Head of College suggested I keep them in his private college garden instead, which I did, and at end of term took them home and gave him some jars of honey for which he thanked me.

Then I joined the navy as a very ordinary seaman, but they made me an officer. I missed being a midshipman by one week. I started to grow a beard to look older, and smoked a pipe. I had a meerschaum, (like Sherlock Holmes) and a briar, plus a corncob. I liked smoking latakia tobacco. Like the other officers at sea I drank gin with drops of angostura bitters (pink gin) but never enough to become tipsy or drunk. After coming off watch late at night I really enjoyed eating Kellogg's corn flakes with canned evaporated milk.

It was not until I was back at university to take another degree that I thought to read the fine print on the evaporated milk can. That's when I discovered it wasn't just evaporated milk I was drinking, but carrageenan as well, which I looked into and found was a substance that had an addictive quality as well as possibly implicated in gastro-intestinal tract inflammation, ulceration and cancer. So I haven't used it from that day to this.

My academic life, such as it was, led me on to a fellowship at the university of Chicago in the US. By then I had given up smoking and had stopped drinking when I left the navy. Now I ate normal food, with the exception of fast food, hot dogs, burgers, prepared meats, pizza, soft drinks, condiments, and such. After about 2 years I decided academic life wasn't for me, and came to Canada. It was obvious Canada didn't need another historian. I thought I would go into business the academic way, as a professional. I didn't want to work with diseases or cut people open, or stand all day working over peoples' bad teeth, or defending criminals in court as their advocate, so decided the independence of an auditor was better, although I hadn't done math since age 14.

It was miserable being really poor and doing audit work. I used to smoke Turkish cigarettes using a black 6-inch long holder. One young student working with me said I looked like a lord of the manor checking his estate accounts. Four years later I became a CA and three years after that started my own practice. That was when my existence really came alive. For the first time I was in charge of my own destiny. So if you're unhappy where you are, working for others, be brave and try working for yourself. During all this time I ate carefully, but normal food as previously mentioned. I was now 38 years old.

The country boy in me hated being cooped up in a city day and night. I tried golf, but was mediocre at it although I chose to frequent a very scenic but difficult course. To satisfy my wish to be a better golfer would require more time than I could spare. The need to swing in a repetitive sudden body twist did not seem good for my back so I dropped golf after a few years. The practice was now taking all my time and in April, tax month, I sometimes had to work right through the night.

By the time I was 50 the high-pressure sedentary life had added 20 lbs to my weight. There was also considerable stress as I now had some quite large and complicated accounts, plus being involved in research, examination and committee work for our Institute. Everyone seemed to want me to do more. I bought a beautiful pale yellow reclining chair and installed it in my personal office. After lunch I would shut the door and try to sleep for 15-20 minutes each day. That was because I had felt faint a few times and suddenly realized that these were mini warnings of a stroke or heart attack to come. This was when the meat industry began injecting animals due for slaughter with chemicals that would make them tenderer when cooked. At first it was printed on the package, and I avoided it, but then the warning notices were dropped so you could not tell whether the meat was injected. But my body could tell. I felt sick after eating meat. So I gave up a lifetime of eating porterhouse and top sirloin steaks and turned to fish instead. From that decision on I have never eaten meat to this day.

I began by eating sockeye salmon steaks. I bought the whole raw fish from a distributor who cut them into steaks for me and said they could no longer get wild salmon. I found that most salmon were being farmed. Instead of leading their natural lives, including roaming the seas as predators and returning with the strength to leap waterfalls on the way to spawning, they were now herded in pens and fed pellets of other waste animal products etc. This unnatural food caused their natural red flesh to turn pale or almost white, so a red dye was added to their food to create a simulated colour. The food these unfortunate creatures were fed must have included fatty material because their underbellies were quite fatty and not regular edible flesh. So I gave up eating salmon, and switched to buying whole halibut instead.

Halibut is a huge bottom feeding flat fish, both eyes on one side of its body. My reason for choosing these to eat was because they are high in protein, which I have always gone for in food as I do mostly brain work, and they had not at that time been successfully farmed. The ones I was buying were wild Alaskan halibut. The distributor cut them in half, head to tail, then into steaks. One fish cost in the hundreds of dollars but lasted me a long time. After a few years of this I read that 2 4D and other noxious chemicals were being found in the Arctic in the bodies of wildlife as well as in the water. Apparently there was mercury on the ocean floor and I was eating a bottom feeder fish. So I reluctantly gave up eating halibut. From that day forward I have not eaten halibut.

You might be interested to know that on March 1st 1999, page 4 of the National Post newspaper in Canada had an article headed "Cabinet allows use of rust to colour ham." The column was a foot long, so here are some extracts: Ottawa (capital city of Canada)

"... Black Forest ham will be showing a bit of rust after a recent change to federal regulations that govern food additives. Cabinet has given the green light to use rust as a new colouring agent for the popular deli meat. Technically the food additive is called iron oxide."... "A meat processing company asked for the change because rust is cheaper and easier to use for colouring ham skins than the caramel the industry used until now...(which)... was bothersome and expensive...It caused condensation in meat coolers and dripped off the hams as they were cooling on racks..."

"Now they can use an edible collagen film...with iron oxide..."

"Collagen is a name for the protein wrap, or skin, on a ham that is derived from animal bones and tendons during meat processing."

"Health Canada has approved the acceptable daily intake of iron oxide at

0.5 milligrams per kilogram of body weight daily...."
Jean Chretien (from Quebec) was prime minister of the (Liberal) government of Canada in 1999.

CHAPTER £
Becoming an auditor

Fortunately my 4 years CA apprenticeship were under a gold medallist, which showed me what the standard could be. Now having a busy and successful auditing and international tax practice I was able to hire silver medallists to do much of the work, though I could never afford or attract a gold. But 10 years after qualifying I was sitting on a dais between two former gold medallists (which of course I was not) my task being to supervise 8 CAs marking the uniform final examination auditing paper across Canada. For 10 days work I was paid about the same as I had earned in my full first year as an apprentice. Even more remarkable was that while at Chicago I had wandered into the

Psychology department with the question could I write a book. During about a week of tests I was told my unspeeded verbal IQ was the maximum - 200. Interest tests showed % interest etc. English 98, history 95, philosophy 94, music 90, business, banking etc. 45. So I was told of course you could write: whatever you do don't go into banking or business. I managed to tweak it into investigative auditing and tax, not accounting or banking, and so survived.

Also, while in Chicago I was invited by visiting T.S. Eliot to lunch, 1 on 1. He told me he couldn't write in the US either, which was why he went to England. He also said regular work, avoided by many writers and poets, was not harmful, quite the reverse. He had worked in a bank for 10 years. For me, there were some temptations along the way. A client got me to talk about social change on a TV station whose manager sent someone to me immediately afterwards with the words 'get him' as they wanted me to do another show for them. And the client wanted me to do tax and federal budget analyses in a program after each change, but somehow TV seemed a deflection from my destined path, though I didn't clearly know what it would be. So I declined these offers. I also noted that one or two successful CAs of my qualification group had developed very large accounting practices and were becoming well known. I thought it was not for me as the profession I was in was not my role in life. Doctors who were tax clients seemed to do well enough, with only a nurse or two and a receptionist. So why expand. The trouble was, the practice kept growing.

I realized I only smoked cigarettes if a client with me did, so I gave up the habit and began drinking and offering clients Twining's teas. The obvious Earl Grey, Darjeeling, Orange Pekoe, English

Breakfast, Prince of Wales, Queen Mary, Chamomile Green Tea, China Oolong, Jasmine Green Tea, Spice, Gunpowder Green, Irish Breakfast, and my favourite, Lapsang Souchong. At first I put milk in with the tea. Then I dropped using milk. That was after I had seen a TV clip showing an unfortunate herd of Holstein cows walking in filth and their own feces.

I had gradually moved up in accommodation from one rented room to an apartment, to a duplex, a rented house and finally owning a house. And from doing my professional work in the duplex, to a one room office to a 2 room office and finally after 6 months negotiations to a small office building. I now had 3 mortgages, but increased equity month by month. Twenty-five years later, they were all paid off.

As the practice had very competent staff now, I read everything that came in, and reviewed all work before it went out, interviewed clients, but no longer did work myself. I had set up 45 item checklist forms to guide staff on each audit or tax return. I now had a young CA in the practice that was previously in the Appeals section of the tax department and a very fine audit specialist CA heading that section of the practice. No one was ever fired, but every applicant wishing to join the firm had to pass a written proficiency test. This also applied to CAs. I happen to think that every candidate for public office should pass a literacy test and be able to reconcile a bank account.

There was more time for other things, as I was not going to expand the practice. I put in long weekday hours at work, so I could free up some spare weekend time. For a number of years I had gone north for summer weekends, camping, and had one particular lake with a park ranger in charge and a far back campsite by a small private lake where I could relax watching turtles sunning themselves. I was always a voracious reader and happened to read the Odyssey by Homer. As a former navy navigating officer, from clues such as star references I could see his voyaging was not where conventional wisdom said it was. I wrote up my conclusions and took them to the Canadian Broadcasting Corporation where I knew nobody. They ran it past a University of Toronto professor who said 'plausible' and I was given a 2 hour radio documentary in their trans-Canada Ideas series. In the program I went to the local planetarium, the director kindly precessed it back to 1200 BC and I was able to quote the text and show the voyage went nowhere near the conventional wisdom. The CBC was astounded at the volume of the public response. I did three more 2 hour documentaries - all investigations of ancient problems - which took about 10 years, by then I'd had enough.

Back to the diet. As a former beekeeper I had never eaten sugar, only unpasteurized honey my entire life. Now that I had given up cooking and eating fish how was I to get high protein. It came about this way. After a few years of camping I began searching for a country property. Eventually I found one. On a highway, with about 1000 feet of frontage; and electricity and telephone passing by. Just a few acres of raw bush, and as a chain of 3 lakes began the other side of the road, not too expensive. My time was still precious, and the contractor who agreed to build me a house didn't show up. My life was based on people doing what they said they would, to the minute. In the city I found I could take evening courses, 3 hours every week for 22 weeks, and chose 4 over 4 years: rough carpentry and house building, dry walling;

bricklaying, tile setting, concrete block laying, rock facing; plumbing and tile bed construction; hydro-electric and house wiring. After the first year I cleared a small site and built a 12x17 ft. cabin, which took 3 years. When I had finished it was fully insulated and winterized with 100 amp electric service.

By working long office hours weekdays and dawn to dusk weekend hours at the country site I was able to put in about 35 hours on each, week by week. This mix of mental and physical work soon stripped off my extra 20 lbs. weight. I learned that hard work did no harm; it was stress that caused tension and physical and mental problems. Now I had somewhere to bake my own bread and gradually shift to becoming a vegetarian.

CHAPTER 3
Potable water

The person I'd bought the country property from said if I couldn't find water on it, I didn't have to buy it. I read up on water divining but was no good at it, so I devised a drill system that would go to about 17 ft. I had a 2" flighted augur brazed on to a 6 ft. length of galvanized pipe, to which I could add extensions, with a T bar at the top end, for turning it.
I found water at one point 13 ft. down. I dug a 36" well shaft, not difficult as it was topsoil, subsoil, then sand, then gravel then hardpan, then rock at 13 ft. I had well tile dropped down it and could then place a ladder in it and go to the bottom if needed. I set up a semi rotary pump, a pipeline to the bottom with a flap valve (non-return valve) so I didn't have to lower buckets down for water.
Then I put a small white metal shed over it, and locked it. Now I had an unlimited

supply of fine sweet potable water to drink, and took a supply back to the city every week.

From this time on I drank nothing but water. No milk, tea, coffee, soft drinks, nothing but well water. The reason was I had read that the city water, which contained chlorine and fluoride, was also adding aluminum sulphate. I had used fluoride toothpaste since I was 20 and did not want to be forcibly fed more fluoride in my water. My understanding was that sodium fluoride tended to cause gouty type arthritis. The aluminum sulphate, I read, was a coagulant, and so useful in water treatment plants for accumulating and disposition of various types of unwanted particles. But it had apparently been implicated in coagulating in the blood of elderly people especially in the brain, with suspected deleterious effects towards Alzheimer's disease.

(Aluminum sulfate (UK PID) www.inchem.org/documents/ukpids/ukpids/ukpid34.htm) I felt much better now that I had this fine clear uncontaminated water to drink. I was then 49 years old.

It took me 18 years of part time industrious effort to complete building on the property. In August of that final year I hung 11 interior doors, and now had a winterized cabin, a 2 car + workshop garage and a house, with all services underground. It was a wonderful place for a writer to be in and the 4 Radio documentaries morphed into 12 surfable books on the Internet. My last was perhaps the longest, The Shakespeare Identity Problem, 36 chapters.

I had always assumed that this property, which I had created from bush would be where I ended my days in this life, but when I was 89 I found I could no longer maintain it. Remarkably, within a few months of making the decision to move into the nearby small town I found there a ground floor condominium unit with a 25 ft. balcony overlooking Lake Huron from a hill top. And a young professional couple had fallen in love with my country property, and bought it. So for me no more concern with finding competent snow removal from driveway or roof tops and no more problem with having exterior maintenance spring, summer and fall. I only mention all this as a background to my explaining that as soon as I found I would need to drink town water, I called the municipal water treatment plant and asked did they put chlorine in the water: yes; did they put sodium fluoride in the water: yes; did they put aluminum sulphate in the water: yes. Anything else: no. I therefore had a reverse osmosis water filtration system installed. It is supposed to remove about 95% or more of these chemicals. So I will have to endure absorbing about 5% of these toxic substances for the foreseeable future.

It so happens that I read Science every week. The 7th Jan 2011 issue p42 had an article by two scientists, one at California, Berkeley, the other at the Swiss Federal Institute of Aquatic Science and Technology, 'The Chlorine Dilemma' which said in part: "Chlorine disinfection has been instrumental in the provision of safe drinking water, but the use of chlorine has a dark side: in addition to inactivating water borne pathogens, chlorine reacts with natural organic matter to produce a variety of Toxic disinfection by-products (DBPs)... These concerns... have recently led many drinking-water andwastewater treatment plants to discontinue the use of chlorine disinfection...the discovery of a potential link betweenDBPsand increased rates of miscarriagesand bladder cancer..."

You can see from this scientific paper that even after having reduced my intake of liquids to nothing but water, my concerns about drinking safe water are not exaggerated.

CHAPTER 4
Bread to eat

Bread seems the next most important food item to discuss.

Earlier I had said I always ate brown bread as a boy, and had to eat what was available at university and in the navy. After that it was always whole wheat or multigrain, as fashions came and went. But once I had good well water and a good health food store only a few miles away I bought stone ground unbleached whole hard wheat flour, kamut flour, spelt flour and amaranth flour. These last 3 are lighter than hard wheat flour.

Kamut is a cereal used by ancient Egyptian civilization about 4000 years ago. It is higher in protein than modern whole wheat. Spelt is a cereal used by ancient European societies about 3500 years ago. When investigating an ancient problem I remember reading that two archaeologists had taken ancient stone sickles and in a half hour reaped enough modern wild descendant cereal-like grasses of spelt that they winnowed and de-hulled and using a pestle and mortar turned into flour and then baked a small loaf of bread with a higher protein content than modern wheat. An amaranth grain is about the size of a pin head. The ancient Greeks thought it had special healing qualities and used it as a symbol of immortality. It was also used by the Chinese for its healing chemicals, curing illnesses such as infections, rashes and migraines. Its protein level is just below that of modern hard wheat. It is a good source of dietary minerals such as iron, phosphorus, and magnesium.

Here's how I baked - and still bake- my bread. I have to admit I no longer stir the mix by hand with a wooden spoon. I now use a 'kitchen centre' with the speed at the minimum and set up with two stainless steel dough hooks in a large stainless steel bowl. You need a measuring cup capacity 1 cup, and a plastic bowl about 11 inches diameter and 4 inches high. From a bag of stone ground whole hard wheat take 6 heaped cupfuls and put into the bowl. Add one cup each of kamut, spelt and amaranth flour. Add two cupfuls of whole wheat bran. The only bran I can get is brown in colour but devoid of weight and I suspect is useless except as a filler or fiber. When I was a boy we used to buy bran as heavy as bread dough that we mixed with water producing a tantalizing aroma, and very tasty to eat. We fed this to the chickens, who loved it. This modern so-called bran seems to have every vestige of nutritious value removed from it, leaving just 'fiber.' I use a plastic strainer with a scoop end having $1/8^{th}$ inch holes in it to stir all these dry ingredients until well mixed. Then keep adding cupfuls to the steel bowl and sparingly add water to the steel bowl.

When about half the mix is in the steel bowl switch on the food processor and so begin turning the mix into dough. Heat some water not too much above lukewarm, put a level teaspoonful of sea salt into a cup and add a little of the warm water, stir a few times and leave to dissolve the salt. In a small preferably transparent plastic bowl put a heaped teaspoon of unpasteurized honey and add the warm water to about 1/3 height of the bowl. Once the honey is completely dissolved add three heaped teaspoonfuls of dry active yeast, shaking each spoonful carefully over the surface of the water to cover the entire surface. While the yeast is working, now add 6 tablespoons of soya oil to the dough being mixed in the steel bowl.

When the salt has dissolved in its container, pour that liquid into the steel bowl as it continues mixing. When the yeast reaches the top of its container, pour the contents into the steel mixing bowl. Continue adding the contents of the flour bowl, until all is transferred.

While the final mixing continues, set out all the pyrex glass containers you calculate you need for the dough, probably, depending on size, some six or eight. Pour the contents from a package of cracked rye into an empty glass jar, be sure the Pyrex containers are at least room temperature, and then gently shake the cracked rye into the bottoms of the Pyrex containers more or less covering them. By now the dough may be the right consistency and well mixed.

Remove the dough hooks, clean and dry, and then using two large plastic ladles; transfer the dough into the waiting Pyrex containers. Do not fill them more than 1/3 full. Place them all in an oven. Then leave for at least 1.5 hours. After a quick check to see that the contents have not spilled over, set the oven to 285 degrees Fahrenheit for 45 minutes. I usually leave them in the oven but turned off until cooled down.

In case you're interested appended is a table showing the relative values of certain nutrients for the four grains mentioned. The information comes from:

http://www.nal.usda.gov/fnic/foodcomp/cgi-bin/list_nut_edit.pl

Value per 100 grams..........................

Nutrient	Unit	Wheat, durum	Kamut
Protein Calcium,	g	13.68	17.30
Ca Iron, Fe	mg	34.00	31.00
Magnesium, Mg	mg	3.52	7.20
Phosphorus, P	mg	144.00	153.00
Potassium, K	mg	508.00	411.00
	mg	431.00	446.00

Nutrient	Unit	Spelt	Amaranth
Protein	g	14.57	13.56
Calcium, Ca	mg	27.00	159.00
Iron, Fe	mg	4.44	7.61
Magnesium, Mg	mg	136.00	248.00
Phosphorus, P	mg	401.00	557.00
Potassium, K	mg	388.00	508.00

CHAPTER 5
Finding high protein

Now that we have given up smoking and imbibing alcohol, drinking only purified water and eating only high protein self baked bread using only unpasteurized honey as a sweetener, this alone will not sustain a satisfactory life style. If we are to avoid all meats and fish we must find suitable heavy duty protein replacements to nourish the body.

It so happened that as I was busily writing my 12 surfable books at my country home the provincial government decided to re-surface the highway passing by it, and in the process cut back the bush to 33 feet from the road along a 1,000 foot frontage. This resulted in the felling or 'dropping' of 86 mature trees: oak, maple, birch, white pine and ironwood. Most of them were 80 - 90 feet tall. The government contractors kindly used their huge shredder to take away all the foliage and limbs they also shredded any saplings under 6 inches in diameter, leaving me the trunks called logs, and large boughs. It took me 2 years of intensive effort to cut the logs into 16 inch so called blocks, roll these on to my driveway, transport them to my parking area, split them with my Honda splitter and then haul the split pieces to storage under my deck in an area 28x8x8ft.

I was already living with a complete vegetarian diet, and wondered as I began this huge task whether I could cope with it when eating only nuts, seeds, beans, cereals, fruit and vegetables. To my surprise I found that I felt in better health and less tired than I used to be doing lighter work at a younger age when eating meat, and later salmon and then halibut. It is because of this surprising discovery that I thought I should write this for you to read in case you wished to follow a similar route to better health.

When I stopped drinking milk that was not all. I already knew that cheese contains about 28% to 40% fat. So I stopped having milk, cheese, butter, and while I was at it, all dairy products and margarine as well.

Eating store-bought dry bread would not be very palatable, but the bread I bake is somehow more moist and I have no trouble eating it as is with fruits, or honey, unpasteurized, of course.

So now after all these comments and explanations we're ready to look at a vegetarian diet, day by day. As you will have seen this was a gradual development. I do not think you can just one day drop your eating habits and switch to what I'm listing here. It seems to me there are enzymes in the human gut that are symbiotic. By that I mean they partially digest the food intake for their own benefit and for their human host's as well. They need to adjust to changes in human diet, and so for better advantage to both parties the changes need to be gradual. But in reporting it for your benefit so as not to drag it out too long, here's the complete weekly menu, as used now for many years:

Monday	
Spelt, Millet, Lentils, Adzuki, Chick	
Tuesday	
Kidney, Navy, Pinto, Mung, Barley	
Wednesday	
Soy, Green Peas*, Lima, Kamut, Chick	
Thursday	
Kamut, Black Turtle Beans, Lentils, Mung, Millet, Green Peas	
Friday	
Quinoa, Adzuki, Short Grain Brown Rice, Lima, Yellow Eyed Peas, Green peas	
Saturday	
Barley, Kidney, Spelt, Pinto, Navy	
Sunday	
Quinoa, Black Turtle Beans, Black Eyed peas, Rice, Soy	

* Whole green peas, not split peas. That's because I found the local town sewage plant was distributing waste product to nearby farmers who were glad to have it free, apparently sprayed on their fields. When I opened a plastic bag of split peas I could smell the sewage in it. Unfortunately human sewage contains residues of various prescription drugs, many of which have serious side effects. The whole green peas come from a different source and smell as peas should.

Green peas make the meal more tasty. Buckwheat (sorghum) is added to any day's meal to thicken it for greater bulk, if needed.

With the ingredients for a meal listed, next we need to explain how to convert this food supply into a meal ready to eat. And this we'll do in the next chapter.

Soy beans and quinoa are both complete proteins. Add one or the other everyday if you wish to increase your protein intake.

CHAPTER 6

Careful measuring

If you think you will just look at Monday's menu, take handfuls of the five listed items, throw them into any old saucepan, boil them up on the stove for a while, let them cool off a bit, then put some in a dish and start eating them, you'll probably break a tooth. I won't presume to tell you how to organize your meals, instead here's how I prepare mine. My present system wasn't born overnight; it gradually evolved over a few years, but has been unchanged for many years now.

First, I have a microwave shelf in the kitchen. I no longer use the microwave because it changes the structure of the food it processes, and the effects are not beneficial. On that shelf there are 22 glass jars 3½" in diameter and 2½" high with metal screw caps on which I placed content labels. The jar contents are kept in alphabetical order. The items come in large packages, so a backup inventory is kept in a nearby cupboard. You will have astutely noticed that I listed only 19 different ingredients in the menus. That's because there are 7 days in the week and buckwheat (sorghum), alfalfa, and amaranth were added later. These can be added from time to time, or used to create the basis for an extra day. But I found an 8 day cycle was awkward to manage.

Monday's list begins with spelt. I use a ¼ cup from a measuring set, place it in a white soup bowl so that the contents will be clearly visible. Next I fill the cup with spelt (cereal) grains. Shake about a fifth into the bowl so that each grain can be seen individually. Nearby is placed a plastic bowl 6" in diameter and 3" deep. Into it are placed any discoloured, misshapen, black spotted, very small, or otherwise different grains. Occasionally some foreign substances such as pieces of similar sized volcanic rock also appear. A brown soya bean is acceptable as some grow that way. The grains that pass the test are emptied into a cooking pot.

The one I use is 6½" wide x3½" deep made of tempered brown glass called Vision which I believe is a French product manufactured under licence by Corning in North America. It can be taken straight from a freezer and put on a hot stove without breaking it, or from a hot stove to a freezer, but it will shatter if hit hard or dropped. It is easy to clean if soaked after use.

The discards collected in the plastic bowl fill it in about a year. In early spring using the corner of a hoe drag it along roto-tilled ground creating a shallow furrow. Gently shake the bowl contents into the furrow (usually good for 30 to 40 feet) then close it by dragging the hoe over it blade down. Miraculously, a fine crop appears in due course, and the product is healthy and good to eat. Unfortunately, deer, woodchuck, raccoons, jack rabbits, voles, mice, and countless insect pests agree. I do not use herbicides, insecticides, fertilizers, and take my chances with the rest of the populace out there.

When all the ingredients for the day which have passed examination are in the saucepan it is filled with water to about 1½" from the top, then stirred back and forth with a plastic ladle about 25-30 times. Any floaters are removed as they have probably been eaten by some pest. The water is then poured off and the process repeated twice. The 4th time the water is brought to about 1¼" from the rim of the saucepan which is now ready to be heated.

For the past 3 years, I have used a single flat top range, with no visible rings and a control knob showing Off, 1,2,3,4,5,Max. I place the saucepan on it and set it to just below 2. This gives a slow warming. After 1½ to 2 hours the control is moved to just under 3, which gives a simmer, not enough to boil over on to the range. After 6-7 hours the range can be turned off and the contents left to cool. Then, at last, the result is ready to be eaten.

Soya beans are important in this diet, as they are complete protein. But now they are genetically engineered (GE). There are two problems with GE soya beans. First, although there is not much difference in food value from natural produce, it is the lack of ability in the plants, bred as they were primarily for high production value, to survive drought, high temperatures, excessive rain storms, and other adverse conditions of nature. Farmers growing

GE crops around the world have found them ruined by weather extremes against which the plants have lost their natural defences. And next, the GE products seem to have less of the pleasant flavour of natural varieties. Years ago I sometimes put a one third cup of soya beans alone in water on a stove and left it there for several hours; they had a pleasant taste when softened and cooked. Not any more, now (GE?) soya beans alone have even a slightly unpleasant taste.

We are all aware now that our field-grown food has been over fertilized, and sprayed with herbicides and pesticides, many of which are systemic, meaning the plant absorbs them into itself from its leaves and the ground it grows in. It may be less known that organic produce has generally been sprayed with Rotenone, permitted in organics because it is derived from natural sources. Here is what Wikipedia had to say January 22, 2012:

Rotenone is an odorless chemical that is used as a broad-spectrum insecticide, piscicide, and pesticide. It occurs naturally in the roots and stems of several plants such as the JICAMA VINE plant. In mammals, including humans, it is linked to the development of Parkinson's disease.... In the United States and Canada all uses of rotenone except as a piscicide |(fish killer) are being phased out.

So, do not think you are escaping insecticides and pesticides by turning to organics. It appears all we can hope to do is make a conscious sustained effort to reduce our intake of these noxious chemicals to a minimum.

After all these explanations and cautions you should now have a meal of high protein ready to eat. But you'll also need fruits and vegetables and that's what we'll discuss in the next chapter.

CHAPTER 7
Fruits and Vegetables

For breakfast I eat a mango with my own baked bread. When buying mangos I examine the top carefully at the slight depression surrounding where it was severed from the tree. If it has black discolouration there it means the fruit is starting to grow rotten inside, or will do so in a few days. This is where excess spraying collects. There is further selection to be made because red skinned mangos are sweeter than green skinned ones. There are two kinds of mangos, the larger ones, just described, and a smaller type (ataulfo), which is yellow and generally sweeter in taste and apparently less prone to overspraying and rot.

Because mangos come from semi-tropical countries, before eating the produce I put on rubber gloves, soft soap the fruit, then wash it off and dry it. That's because I have no idea as to the cleanliness of the hands of pickers or sorters in far off lands, or what might be the risk of their possible carrying of tropical or semi-tropical diseases. Next, I use a (potato) peeler and peel the mango from top to bottom all around, place it in a soup bowl and eat it with a knife and fork. They generally come with hard texture, but soften after 2 or 3 days on top of the refrigerator.

My next, midmorning, snack is generally to eat two (preferably organic, which are less harmfully sprayed and taste better) bananas, with my own bread. I have read that wild bananas are poisonous to humans and all commercial edibles are grafts from one particular stalk. Apparently a disease has begun to attack these grafts and has become almost impossible to eradicate. There were even predictions that the days of edible bananas were numbered. That was some years ago and I still see plenty of bananas in stores, so perhaps the problem was overcome. I have noticed that regular store-bought bananas have tended to become stringy in their centre cores, which is why I switched to organics that were good to eat. More recently I find even organic bananas seem 'dead' and lack their former good taste and I am reducing their use. Replacing them as an important food source is still an ongoing problem.

Because I eat small meals fairly frequently, after another two hours or so I might eat a potato. I prefer the red skinned variety, which after some experimentation I found were the most tasty (in my opinion). My procedure with potatoes is to put 5 in a Visions saucepan 8" wide x 4" deep and cover them with water. Set the stove range top to medium (6 o'clock) until you hear them boiling, and then reduce the heat to 9 o'clock. After about 45 minutes the range can be turned off. A sharp knife inserted into one potato should pass through it cleanly with no residue on the knife, indicating it is cooked through. When cooled I place each in a Ziploc plastic bag in the frig., not the freezer. To eat, place one potato in the usual soup bowl, slice into halves lengthwise, and then quarters, preferably peeling off the skin. Then pour a teaspoonful of soya oil on each quarter. This is because there is no butter or margarine or cheese or other fat in the menu.

You will probably want to eat green vegetables with the potato. You might like 6 or7 slices of an English cucumber, so called, I know not why. An alternative would be several leaves from a Romaine, Boston or Leaf type lettuce. The problem with the lettuce is that every wild creature or insect loves lettuce so it is sprayed relentlessly. Even washing it thoroughly is no good as the sprays are systemic. Personally I do not like broccoli, although claimed to be very beneficial to health. Kale and collard greens are high in calcium and are alternative greens, smelling less pungent than broccoli or cabbage or Brussels sprouts while being cooked Whatever greens you choose should be washed carefully as all are heavily sprayed and at least some surface spray can be removed. What I do with kale or collard greens after boiling until a fork will easily penetrate it, is divide it into sections, and place each in a Ziploc freezer bag and store these in the freezer. The bag contents can then be added one by one to beans etc. main meals.

Another vegetable is butternut squash. I prefer the long ones as the bulbous head is full of seeds. This I prefer to bake in the oven in a Pyrex long dish with a 300 degree heat for about 45 minutes, depending on size. Sweet potatoes I slice lengthwise and when cooled eat by themselves as a snack. Parsnips can be eaten with greens and other vegetables, I suggest. I peel parsnips with the potato peeler before cooking. They can be added in with sweet potatoes for boiling in the 8" Visions saucepan.

Fruits eaten other than bananas and mangos are mainly apples, cherries and oranges. The apples are organic Gala or yellow delicious. All supermarket apples seem to be about twice or three times the size of the natural unfertilized ones as a boy I used to eat sitting up in apple trees watching my bees below. About 3 years ago I read of a doctor in a famous pediatric clinic who said children should not eat more than one apple a day as they were so heavily sprayed.

The cherries I am eating now (January) are from Chile. These come in transparent plastic Ziploc bags. There are no under ripe or overripe or rotten contents. I suspect they may have been irradiated to lengthen the shelf life. If so, then the enzymes will have been killed and so a natural benefit lost. About 15 - 20 are placed in a colander and reverse osmosis tap water run over them for a minute or so, before drying in a small towel and then ready to enjoy. But they are heavily sprayed.

Oranges eaten are preferentially juice types. They are eaten for the juice, not the taste. Out of season these come from South Africa. A sharp knife is run around the circumference no deeper than the peel in two different directions, and then the peel is removed. The remaining white interior is opened into its natural sections and these are separated and eaten one by one.

You will have noticed that this diet does not include any condiments such as salt, pepper or other more exotic additives.

Because there is no meat of any kind in this diet we next need to talk about supplements, and this we'll do in the next chapter.

CHAPTER 8
Supplements

Vitamin B12 is an essential part of this diet. The requirement per day is only 25 mcg so why take more. Excessive amounts of vitamins and other additives have apparently been found to cause contrary effects and are even suspected of causing cancer. I always buy the lowest mcg or mg I can get, Jamieson because it says natural sources, no salt, no sugar, no starch, no gluten, no lactose, which gives an idea as to what some other products may contain.

In 2014 the lowest vitamin B12 tablet obtainable is 100 mcg. So I now take 1 tablet Monday, Wdnesday and Friday.

I used to get capsules, but read that a woman in England who was a vegetarian developed mad cow disease. This mystified the local medical profession until it was found that the soft components of the exterior gel of the capsules she swallowed contained boiled up remains of cattle indiscriminately collected, diseased included. From then on I pierced the capsules and swallowed the contents, throwing out the soft empty capsules.

The 16 March 2012 issue of Science page 1280 had the following item:

Medicine
Bone of Contention Vitamin E is a widely used dietary supplement because its antioxidant activity is thought to benefit cardiovascular health. As is true for many supplements, vitamin E's health effects are complex; its role in bone metabolism has been particularly controversial. Two

independent studies support the view that the form of vitamin E used in most supplements (α-tocopherol) may adversely affect bone. Fujita *et al,* found that mice lacking α-tocopherol transfer protein, a model of vitamin E deficiency, had a higher bone mass than controls, because of reduced activity of bone-resorbing cells called osteoclasts. Wild type mice fed a diet supplemented with α-tocopherol showed a 20% reduction in bone mass as compared to controls; however, the mice were young and undergoing rapid bone growth, so the relevance to effects in adult humans is uncertain. However, data derived from a cross- sectional study of postmenopausal women, about half taking vitamin E, are broadly consistent with the mouse work. Association between serum levels of α-tocopherol, γ-tocopherol, and markers of bone formation and turnover in the women led Hamidi *et al*, to postulate that vitamin E

supplements may negatively affect bone formation–PAK
Nat.Med. 18, 10.1038/mm.2659 (2012); J.BoneMiner. Res.27,10.1002/jbmr.1566 (2012).

I no longer take vitamin E supplements.

Monday and Thursday
Wakame - (actually a form of cultivated and dried kelp)

This expands exponentially when placed in a glass of water. When expanded, taken from the glass with a fork and dropped on top of a bowlful of cooked beans of the day. Wakame is eaten raw. Local kelp, called dulse, was tried but found to have sand particles so wakame was reverted to instead. It is an excellent source of calcium.

Saturday
B6 1 x 50 mg
B3 (Niacin) No-Flush. With Inositol.

The smallest Niacin dose I can get is 500mg replacing the 100 mg I used to buy. So now I have settled for half, (250 mg) as the tablets are scored. As it is only taken once a week, this will have to do for the present. The no flush is important. Once some years ago in another town I bought a different brand of Niacin. After taking a tablet my face and next my whole skin area seemed to become red and flushed. I had no idea what was happening to me, and it was over an hour before it began to subside. I thought I had been poisoned and threw out the bottle of Niacin.

Monday to Saturday:
8 swallows of concentrated orange juice.

I buy (living in Canada) President's Choice 100% pure frozen concentrated orange juice pulp free (PC). This is the only product I have found that actually tastes like orange juice that one juices oneself from a fresh orange. But even this product says in the fine print:

INGREDIENTS: concentrated orange juice, water.

Years ago an American company called Old South had the best, unadulterated orange juice. But its equipment became old, and it sold out to McCain's who promptly increased the price and added water. My problem with adding water is not only the adulteration. Is it just tap water? How pure is it? What percentage is added? There is no answer to these legitimate questions.

Once I have taken the metal top off a PC container I replace it with a plastic sandwich bag held in place with an elastic band and keep the container in the fridge. It is empty after about 3-4 days.

Do not swallow the concentrate without first drinking about ½ a glass of water. Then the juice goes down without burning your throat (esophagus) and you are saved the trouble of mixing it with water, as your stomach will do this for you.

Monday – Saturday
Cod liver oil. I used to buy a 500 ml plastic container and swallow about a tablespoonful or slightly more direct from the bottle each morning. This is an important source for vitamins A and D. Unfortunately cod liver oil is no longer available in my region. Instead I take A and D capsules Monday, Wednesday and Friday. I bit the capsules open, suck out the contents and discard the empty capsule.

The various vitamin additives are taken soon after getting up in the morning.

CHAPTER 9
Nuts, bees and drugs

There has been no mention of nuts. Almonds have been described as the king of nuts, so why bother with anything else. They are a good source of calcium, however quite expensive to buy. I used to chew up raw almonds in my mouth, whole, until one day I broke a tooth, and had to have the remains painfully extracted. Now I put them through a blender, after washing them 3 times by shaking them up in a sealed plastic tub and then drying them in a small towel. The blender has 7 active settings and I use 'chop' for the almonds. I eat a few spoonfuls over the course of a week.

As a former beekeeper I am naturally concerned to read that honeybees appear to be suffering whole colony sudden death. Almond tree orchards are one place relying on beekeepers placing hives there when the trees blossom, for their mutual benefit. In my day aconite disease was something to guard against for the bees, and when at university I gave a few of my bees to a fellow graduate who was a parasitical proto zoologist, later becoming a professor there. Fortunately he reported back that they were completely healthy.

To return to the present. I realize it is commonly thought that some disease or other is afflicting the bees, but I think it is more likely to be due to the enormous predilection for spraying everything with noxious chemicals that doesn't give the bees a fair chance to live their lives.

About 15 years ago I bought a small container of Roundup and sprayed some on a flourishing dandelion plant growing at the edge of a walkway. The weed collapsed at once and began to shrink in agony. Within a few days it was just a small black skeleton. Later I noticed on Prairie TV advertisements for Roundup ready crop seeds or grains. This I understood to mean that if the subsequent crops were sprayed with Roundup while growing they would not die as the dandelion had done. I also read that small birds had been found dead in cornfields as they had tried to eat from corncobs. From that time forward I have not eaten corn and have bought organic kamut grain and organic stone ground whole hard wheat flour for my bread.

About 30 years ago I bought a pressurized can of a pesticide for use in killing wasps as I had a hornets' nest between the soffit and fascia of my house. I waited until after dark and then sprayed their entrance as far in as I could direct the spray. It only took a few minutes but there were no more wasps. The can warnings said the contents should be kept away from hands, face, pets, and water. A few years later I read that it was now banned. New Zealand farmers had used it in sheep dips. It had spread to wells, poisoned them and the wells could not be cleared of the poison. It was a very virulent chemical.

In another unrelated incident I read of a doctor who had moved from elsewhere to a practice in Summerside in Prince Edward Island province in Canada. He noticed a statistically significant increase in cancer victims over the number in his previous practice. He attributed this to the spraying of crops as where he now practised was a farming area.

This reminded me of a successful farmer I had as a client in my practice. He once told me he put on special waterproof protective clothing when he went out to drive his equipment spraying his crops. He never allowed his family to eat his field crop produce, but kept a small private garden next to his house where he grew his own unsprayed vegetables.

Drugs in one form or another are into everything, either prescribed or over the counter, legal or illegal. All drugs have side effects. Even aspirin is a blood thinner and can cause stomach upset. When a family member entered a retirement home she had not had any medication in over 30 years. The home's doctor quickly began prescribing and she now is taking 5 different drugs. It's the culture we live in. Who ever heard of a dog dying of cancer, but that's what happened to a pet belonging to a junior member of the family. That's because the animal food is cast offs of the same food as humans eat, with the same consequences and they are basically treated with the same drugs.

Cleanliness has extended our life span, but the food we eat and what it contains is killing us prematurely. Humans have the potential to live about 120 years, but we are not fulfilling our potential.

In these few chapters you now have sufficient information to enable you to change your life style and eat less, and healthily. It should be a gradual, not a catastrophic change. Remember, your abdomen is home to many parasites that are beneficial, in a symbiotic relationship. They help process your food and feed themselves as well. They have to adjust to food changes they are not used to processing.

CHAPTER KO
The end of Bees

As a youth bees fascinated me. I read everything I could find about them, including a huge American book 'The ABC and XYZ of beekeeping.' Then I read about Gregor Mendel's work not only with genetics and peas but also with honeybees. He had produced a hybrid strain, which provided much excellent nectar for honey, but was also vicious and stung everyone for miles around, it was said. I had a similar experience. I had read that Dutch bees were very prolific, so I imported a Dutch queen. When the bees started multiplying, which they certainly did, they became unmanageable. I had never worn a veil or gloves, just smoked a cigarette (without inhaling) or used a smoker. But I could not get near the Dutch bees without being stung, not just once but by multiple attacks. I simply had to get rid of them.

My fascination with bees was not just for the saleable honey they kindly provided; it was because they were completely well organized social societies. I wondered how they worked. Who decided when they should swarm? How was it decided when they should build a queen cell and feed the larva 'royal jelly' to make another queen? Who decided or how did they decide which should stand in the entrance way fanning the hot moisture laden air out of the hive and fresh air in? Who decided when a born bee should cease to be a nursemaid and start foraging? How was it arranged that some bees were born from unfertilized eggs and so became male drones? How did they decide who should be making more hexagonal cells from wax, who should go gathering nectar, and who get pollen? Was the queen the director, or did they even have a controller? They never fought in the hives. The whole society operated with extreme efficiency and there was never warfare between hive populations. These were just tiny insects, yet they had some form of advanced civilization. They had been in existence for apparently hundreds of millions of years. Humans only seemed to become agriculturalists instead of hunter-gatherers about 12,000 years ago and only developed 'civilized' societies with cities comparable to bee colonies about 5,000 years ago.

All this took place in my life more than 70 years ago. But naturally, when I had completed building my country home many years later, in a different country, I bought a bee hive and populated it with racks of foundation comb and a stock of bees. They did well and by June probably had 40 or more pounds of honey. Then a bear came. I heard it screaming as it ran past my open bedroom window at 3 am. It had smashed the hive to pieces, ripped out and scattered the comb on the ground, eaten much of it, bees and wax included. The bees next day found a hollowed out piece of trunk in a live tree, probably created by a woodpecker or a flicker, and they migrated there. But in those days January temperatures sometimes dropped at night to 40 degrees below zero fahrenheit and the bees did not survive.

Back to the present, and my reading of Science, 20th April 2012 journal. There were two scientific reports on bees. One was about honeybees. A brief abstract of their report said:

Non-lethal exposure of honeybees to thiamethoxam (neonicotinoid systemic pesticide) causes high mortality due to homing failure at levels that could put a colony at risk of collapse. Simulated exposure events on free-ranging foragers labelled with a radio-frequency identification tag suggest that homing is impaired by thiamethoxam intoxication. These experiments offer new insights into the consequences of common neonicotinoid pesticides used worldwide.
(Science 20 April 2012 Vol 336 #6079 pps348-350).

The abstract of the other report said:

Growing evidence for decline in bee populations has caused great concern because of the valuable ecosystem services they provide. Neonicotinoid insecticides have been implicated in their decline because they occur at trace levels in the nectar and pollen of crop plants. We exposed colonies of the bumblebee *Bombus terrestrios* in the laboratory to field-realistic levels of the neonicotinoid imidacloprid, and then allowed them to develop naturally under field conditions. Treated colonies had a significantly reduced growth rate and suffered an 85% reduction in production of new queens compared with control colonies. Given the scale of use of neonicotinoids, we suggest that they may be having a considerable negative impact on wild bumblebee populations across the developed world. (Science 20 April 2012, Vol 336 No 6079 pp351-352).

Why am I telling you all this? Because if you, like me, no longer use sugar, which has been implicated in the spreading of type 2 diabetes, and instead use natural honey bought from a health food store, then we are still at risk. That's because those honey bee foragers that successfully take back nectar to their hives place it in honeycombs where it is evaporated off to produce honey. That must concentrate the systemic residue traces of these insecticides, which we are subsequently ingesting. So it seems we cannot entirely escape the consequences of misguided 21st century crop-growing practices.

Since it probably has had a significant positive effect on my well being for at least about 80 years of my life, I should mention my relationship with music. It all began when my 20-year-old mother fell in love (or so she thought) with a French concert pianist. Her parents would not permit the marriage. She could play keyboard reasonably well and liked the compositions of Chopin. Instead, at 22 she married my father, a retiring Navy Officer twice her age. It so happened that he had a fine piano. It was a happy marriage. I was the only child. I never heard a cross word between them. So now you know why I had to spend the first 16 years of my life literally glued to the keyboard of a family piano. I passed all the exams of the Associated Boards of the Royal College and Royal Academy of Music: Primary, Elementary, Intermediate, Advanced and Final (with Honours) and then had to take my LRAM degree

(Performers). The 2 theoretical parts were easy enough, then came the practical.

My Academy tutor said he could get me (age 16-17) through the Teachers OK but doubted that I could pass the Performers. He said of one piece (Chopin) I was playing 'I played this at Wigmore Hall last night', sat down at the piano and played the first few bars of Chopin's Polonaise in A Flat. I could only dream of playing like that. For my practical LRAM exam I played the Chopin, Bach Prelude and Fugue Book 2, Opus 22, and Beethoven's The Tempest sonata Opus 31 #2. It didn't help that I broke my right arm doing high jump at school about a month earlier. The examiner failed me 'not without musical ability' he wrote. I would have failed anyway. I did not have sufficient manual dexterity.

Here's what I mean by manual dexterity. If you were to listen to a great deal of Haydn's music, and even play it, I think you might conclude he tinkles along squeezing every drop out of minimal invention. It was not very demanding music to perform. He died in 1809. In that same year was born

Frederic Chopin. Instead of a 66-note he was blessed with an 88-note keyboard and he used every inch of it. If you listen to his Prelude No.16 or better, play it, you attack the first six full stretch chords hammering them out with all the fury you can generate, then race as fast as you can possibly go to complete three pages of sheet music in 54 seconds or less. I could not do this in less than about 58 seconds. Chopin's 4 Ballades and Scherzos are almost equally demanding. And it is not just those two composers but each and every one has a personalized way of putting themes, chords, tonality, rhythm, colour and form together.

So for the rest of my life I have lived almost always to an accompaniment of classical music. As I write this I am listening to the playing of baroque music, which I like most, as I regard Johann Sebastian Bach as the greatest composer who has ever lived. I can listen to any of his music all day and enjoy it. This I cannot do, for example, with Beethoven, whose mother died of tuberculosis and whose father was an alcoholic. Beethoven himself apparently suffered from lead poisoning and possibly syphilis. For me the suffering in his life is borne out in his music and I cannot live with this all day. Although I spend most of my life alone, I never feel lonely, as I am surrounded by elegant music.

I have a warning for you. When you become about 80 years of age be careful what you try to lift. I learned this lesson the hard way. Back during the time when I was cutting up, hauling, splitting and stacking the 86 trees the Highway Department had left for me to deal with, towards the end I cut an oak trunk that was about 15 inches across and of course I cut it into about 16-18 inch lengths. Without thinking I reached down to lift it into my small trailer to haul up the driveway to the splitter. It was very heavy and I had a struggle to put it in the trailer. I continued with the day's work without further incident. The next morning when I woke up and tried to move to get out of bed, I was in agony. I could not move without searing pain. It took me about an hour just to get successfully out of bed. Over the next few days the pain gradually subsided, but I realized I had herniated a disc in my back. The displaced disc was now pinching a major nerve in my spinal column. I could do nothing except barely feed myself, go to the bathroom, and find a way to sit or partially lie down. It was about two full weeks before the pain subsided enough for me to lead a normal life and about a month more before I could resume my usual lifestyle with no pain or weakness. From then on for about two years I was quite careful about what I did and how I used my body. Until then I had never in my life even thought about my physical self. What my mind had decided I should do, I just went ahead and did. Now I had to be more careful.

When I was about 84 it became increasingly difficult to start my tractor and walk-behind lawnmower by hand. So I bought a John Deere walk-behind self-propelled lawn mower with electric start, and a garden tractor with a mowing deck and electric start.

This allowed me to continue maintaining the exterior of the property from April to October each year.

But another problem arose. When I was 83 I decided that my reactions on the road when I was driving were not what they had been, I was no longer a completely defensive driver. Not wishing to cause an accident after 66 years with an unblemished record I took my car off the road and no longer renewed my driver's licence. The problem that now arose was that I was living 16 miles from the nearest town and needed weekly groceries and other usual supplies. A kind friend who passed my home on the way into town would get my grocery list by phone and drop these supplies off on the way past when going home. Occasionally I was offered a ride into town. This arrangement was very limiting though, as I did not wish to ask for too much and I have always lived a very independent life.

By the time I was 86 I realized that I could no longer maintain the property even with electric start equipment. My annual harvesting of wood had dropped almost to nil, and the scything of an acre or so had become too much for me. Nor could I get competent help.

My little parcel of bush land had been over the years turned into a small country estate. There were no leaning trees or fallen ones. These had all been cut up, carted away and burned as winter firewood in my two high efficiency wood-burning stoves. The property was in prime condition for a sale. But I had never thought I would have to leave it. I had always assumed I would be carried away from it eventually, feet first. Now I had to realize that if it was not sold in the next year or two at the most, its exterior condition would deteriorate. It had served a wonderful purpose and helped me create 12 surfable books. Once the inevitability of this plain truth had sunk in, I had to initiate a search for a suitable buyer, and myself find a place to live in the nearby little town, which happened to be set on the east shore of Lake Huron. All this took longer than expected.

It was not until I was 89 that all the selling and buying arrangements were completed.

That was 2½ years ago. I can assure you from personal experience that no matter how entrenched you are in your present position, lifestyle, or residence and neighbourhood, when the time comes for a transition to something else, if you do your 'due diligence' to research for your next move, you will never regret the change, once made. In my case I now have a scooter to travel around town. I have easy access to two supermarkets, a Walmart superstore, Home Depot, 4 major banks, my doctor's office (which I visit about once every 5 years or so), a regional hospital if needed, and trouble free conditions at now 92 years old as I complete this final chapter in my short little book. So a change in venue has not impaired in any way, (I hope) my propensity to write. Finally, then, good luck in all you do, I hope what you have read here has been helpful to you.

END

Made in the USA
San Bernardino, CA
12 December 2014